Bright Minds Empty Souls

By Jennae Cecelia

Bright Minds Empty Souls

Second Edition

ISBN: 978-1541234758

For L-

*Without you, these poems would merely be
papers scattered around my room in messy
handwriting and worn down journals.
Thank you for inspiring me everyday
to be the best me.*

Dear Reader,

Writing has always been the easiest way for me to communicate with others. Whether it was passing notes with friends, or sharing my inner secrets with pen to paper.

Over the course of six years I have written the poems that make up this book. Some started out on napkins from Starbucks, others on the sheets of homework I should have been doing instead.

My advice to you is don't be afraid to face your problems head on. Don't question if your passions are what you should be pursuing. Don't be afraid to love unconditionally.

Bright Minds Empty Souls is for the hopeless romantics and those who need a friend to comfort their late night thoughts. It's a book made with love about falling in and out of love with yourself, and others.

I hope you enjoy reading this as much as I enjoyed writing it.

With Love,

Jennae

Instant Gratification

She didn't need instant gratification,
or want some short-term fling.
But the world was piled
with people looking to
"feel good"
for only a brief moment.
Fast food,
instant coffee,
microwave dinners.
Anything to cut time
and make it easier.
She wasn't about to settle for
cheap food
and mediocre coffee,
so why would she settle for your need
of instant gratification?

Cream In My Coffee

I stopped putting cream in my coffee
because the more I put in,
the less it resembled
your beautiful
brown
eyes.

Commitment Issues

I was so afraid of commitment
that I couldn't even
write in pen.
The thought of a permanent
creation with no way to erase it
was overwhelming.

Air

If someone asked me to pick
you or air,
I would pick you every time.
What ia worth having air to breathe
if I can't breathe it with you?

How To Love

I was never good at loving
moderately.
Either loving
too much,
or too little.
There was no happy medium.
You either had every bit of
my attention,
or none of it at all.

Stranger

I spilled my secrets out to you
through written messages and calls.
Told you who I wanted to be,
and what scared me most of all.
But then you let me go.
Now you're just a stranger
who knows everything I know.

Problem

The problem this time was
I didn't stay quiet like the rest.
And you hated someone who
talked back with a voice
louder than yours.

Look At Me

You looked at me the same
whether my face showed
my artistic skills or
displayed scars
from pimples I picked
as an adolescent.
To you,
I was a work of art
in every form.

Memory

It is a blessing and a curse
to remember everything.
Remember all the details,
like the songs we used to sing.
When I try to push those moments
to the back of my mind.
It just takes one single note,
to bring them back to life.

Toy

Just like a child does with a new toy,
you played with me for awhile
and then forgot about me
when something better came along.

Taste of Your Name

I hate how when I say your name now
it isn't the same flavor as before.
It's tainted by the taste
of bad decisions
and heartbreak.

I hate how when I hear your name now
it doesn't trigger a smile.
It punctures my ears with a nuclear effect.
Who knew a name could mean so much.
Who knew four letters of the alphabet could
make or break my day.

Nothing is better than your eyes locked to
mine.
The feeling of your arms around my body
and your light kisses pressed against my
forehead.
The way you walk into a room with
confidence and have everyone admiring
your ever-present alluring aura.
Makes me wonder how I got so lucky to
have the person they all want to know.
I'm the one who gets to hear all the
brilliant thoughts of that mind.
Get to see you unedited.
It's hard to find any imperfections in the
person you love.
Maybe that's how you still wanted my
Sunday morning makeup smeared face.
Or still loved me even with the stretch
marks on my naked body.
I never felt weird showing you the places
others only guess about.
And you made me feel like nothing
compared to it before.

Emptiness

I didn't know what emptiness felt like until you
took happiness out of my mind,
kindness out of my heart,
and beauty out of my eyes
with the toxic,
gray clouds
that made up your soul.

Anxiety

I have a bad habit of stumbling over my
words and turning red when I am talking.
My hands start to sweat and my voice
sounds like vomit trying to escape.
I am silenced by the awkward stares and
whispers hinting at mean comments.
But please don't mistake my anxiety as me
being unfriendly.

Just Touch It

Touch my soul.
It's bare and vulnerable.
Touch my hands.
They are embedded with fear.
Touch my spirit.
Just so you can crush it.

Vacant

My spot in your life became vacant.
Like a help wanted sign
on the outside of a store.
A new employee to fill the position.
I wasn't needed anymore.

Laughter

Every time you laughed
I felt as if our souls were going to get
a few more months of life in the end.
Because experiencing your laugh was like
taking a dose of prescription happiness.

Not a Home

People feed off of sadness because they
are afraid of happiness.
Afraid of having that fire be lit inside
them only to get blown out by a brief
disturbance.
Afraid the smile that was once effortless
will be forced in place by clenched teeth.
Sadness may be an emotional state to
think and reflect,
but it is no place to give up at and make
your home.

Wine

I can feel this wine going right to my
head,
and you are heading straight for my
heart.

Lunch Break Confession

If you had said goodbye maybe this would
have hurt less.
Closure,
we lacked closure.
One morning it's, "hello"
and the next nothing.
Your breath stopped, and your heart
didn't race when I was near.
Everyone said your name in a whisper
because saying it too loud might make it
real.
Maybe I should have said hello back so
that you could have said goodbye.

Tea

I wasn't your cup of tea because you wanted to
add
cream
and sugar
and couldn't just take me as I was.

Waiting

I couldn't wait in a line that took longer
than 20 minutes.
I couldn't wait for the commercials to stop
playing between *One Tree Hill*.
I couldn't wait for much at all because my
patience was so slim.
But some how I spent years waiting for
you and I'll keep waiting until the end.

Cold Turkey

I couldn't say goodbye to you so soon
and with no explanation.
I couldn't just stop our conversations
and silly notes to one another.
Being lead down a road with
no warning signs ahead.
It was like I was abruptly met with a cliff
and I continued to fall.
I couldn't just quit you cold turkey.

Numb

I need Novocain around my heart,
so that I can't feel the pain of longing for
you as you drill into my core.

Human

Imperfections made up her body.
Little red dots,
and stretch marks from growth.
She lived in a world that fell more attracted to
the women who looked like they spent
their days lying out on the beach.
But you connected her freckles on her body
and made them into constellations.
You kissed the marks along her hips.
Imperfections to you were
what made her yours.
Because you knew everything
her body had was because
she was human.
The best human.

Tears

You told her that her eyes looked a
beautiful shade of blue when they were
filled with tears.
So tears were all she made,
just to feel you near.

Shades

Purple.
Lavender and amethyst.
Colors that made up total bliss.
When I see these colors
in the sky at night or
in the morning.
I think of how shades of purple
were all that you were made up of.

Inked

She spilt ink over you.
Wrote about you until her hands had blue
ink in each crevice and her fingers would
leave visible fingerprints.
Her fingers hurt the next morning from
endless printing of letters traced with
your name.
She went through 18 sticky notes trying to
describe your smile.
But you didn't know how many ways she
tried to explain your mannerisms.

Patience

There were very few minds that
I wanted to explore.
Some call it pickiness.
I call it patience.

True Feelings

What a world it would be
if everyone wore their hearts
on their sleeve.
Feelings displayed for all to see.
No questions about
people's sanity or
what their intentions might truly be.

Spoiled

Even the best flavor
can be spoiled
by the taste
of a bitter memory.

Settling

Don't settle.
Be with someone who
wants to hold you hand,
and give you forehead kisses.
Someone who will drive long distances
just to spend a few hours with you.
Don't settle.
Be with someone who will
make you feel loved 365 days.
Someone who says, "us" and not, "me"
when speaking of future plans.
Don't settle.
You're better than that.

Goddess

She wasn't a goddess
to say the least.
With a mind of passion
and colorful thoughts,
she made her way through a world
filled of self-absorbed people.

The Answer

She looked at him with eyes
over flowing with joy.
She wondered how anyone before her
had ever let him go.
That there was someone out there
regretting the hand they dropped.
Regretting not getting to hear his laugh.
Regretting giving up on him.
That same person probably wonders
who is making him happy now.
The answer is, me.

Future

I find myself 12 steps ahead.
Living more in the future than the present.
Reminiscing on the past.
Worrying about what's ahead.
Dreading what I have left behind.
Forgetting to remember.
Remembering all I have forgotten.
I hope tomorrow is a better day.
Because here I am today still thinking of
everything but what is in front of me.

People Always Leave

I took a deep breathe into your cotton
shirt to remember every bit of your
woodsy scent.
We parted ways even though I was still
lingering onto your body.
Afraid of what might never be again.
Your Chevy truck roared to a start and
we snuck one last kiss through
your open window.
And that was the last time I saw you.
Because people always leave.

Blank Canvas

Here I am
with a blank canvas.
All the options spread out
in front of me.
But I can't pick up the brush
with a shaky hand.
I am afraid of only reaching for
the dark colors and repeating
a project I have put to rest.
I want to start fresh.
Start new.
That's why I'm keeping it
a blank canvas.

Bright Minds

His mind was
bright
but his soul was
empty.

Unknown Fear

You said that the ocean scared you
because of all the immense unknown
that existed within it.
Now I know why you couldn't be
committed to me,
because I was vast like an ocean
with deep wisdom and strength.
And I scared you.

Messes of Me

I bet you find bits of me
all around your house.
The comb I left in your drawer.
Little notes I left around for you.
A coffee mug permanently stained
with my lipstick.
I am sure you are still plucking my
hair off of your shirts,
or sink,
or shower.
I wonder how it is so easy for you to look
over these things and not think of me.
Because I can barely keep from crying
if I hear your name.

Fixing

I loved all the broken pieces
because I found beauty in fixing things.
Even those shattered upon repair.
But you were the type to destroy it all
again a few moments after spending
months completing it.

Live

Are we surviving
or are we living?
Although the two may be synonyms,
they don't mean the same.
For one will leave you dried out
and hateful
and the other will make you abundant
and beautiful.
Live, don't just survive.

99 Wrinkles

Because when she is 99 with wrinkles
and her outer appearance has shifted,
you'll remember her in her green eyes
and the passion behind them.

Deeply Please

She was a simple soul
made up of words only written
late at night.
Who could barely ever get her hair
or makeup right.
But her outer appearance
was only a small sample
of who she really could be.
Because her heart was huge and she
loved the mess out of anyone
she cared to deeply please.

Rose Thorns

My love for you was in
the simple things like dried roses.
Moments in time that were frozen.
Although covered with thorns,
their beauty shines through.
Showing you that to get to
the best part the hard times
come too.

Books of You

Because of you I have a reason to write
that isn't about melancholy thoughts.
You are the inspiration for my writing.
Every poem, story and plot.
You are the one I write for.
I write because of your existence.

Shades of Love

They met through shades of
oranges
and
yellows.
All the beautiful colors made them up.
The sunrise in the morning,
and the time just before dusk.
The fall leaves,
and spring flowers.
Years of colorful times
only felt like hours.
As the seasons change,
the two of them grow together.
Through the worst and the best of the
weather.

Shadows

I was the shadow you could never catch.
Always right there with you
but a step ahead.
Casting images in front of your eyes,
only to disappear when it gets dark.

2:16

My eyes always seem to wander
to the clock when the time is 2:16.
It is no coincidence at all,
because I bet it's the same time you are
missing me.

The Worst Pain

Tell me why my heart hurts
when you are still here.
I have the learned the worst pain
I can feel is someone breaking my heart.
Because unlike when someone dies,
I still know you are out there.
Only a phone call,
or car ride away.
That's the pain that will live inside me.
Knowing there is a chance I could have
made a change.

You're Off

I can feel you slipping away.
The desire for me has faded from
your mind.
Your ever-present hand in mine
has turned to a phantom touch.
I miss it.
I miss how it used to be.
What did I do to make me be
the last thing on your mind?

Who is This?

I see him after all of this time
and I don't even recognize the
5 o'clock shadowed face in front of me.
The spaces between his fingers now have
replaced my hand with a lit cigarette.
His bright blue eyes I once knew are
bloodshot and dark circled.
His laugh is now masked with
a deep and repeated cough.
Who is this boy in front of me?
Not the person I thought he was.

I Belong to You

Part of me will always belong to you.
You are inside of me forever.
Running through the cells in my body.
You are the spark behind my eyes.
I don't think I would ever be able to
fully give my heart to someone else
and maybe that isn't fair.
But sometimes a love like ours isn't
supposed to stop just because one
person took a different path.

Don't Even

Don't look at me
with the eyes that gazed at her.
Don't talk to me
with the mouth that was locked
to her lips.
Don't smell my perfume
with the nose that inhaled her.
Don't come to me
when you are sick of her.

Childhood

I miss the sidewalk chalk days,
and the endless games of hide and seek.
When the last thing we wanted were the
streetlights to come on because that
meant a good day coming to an end.
I miss the days of picking dandelions until
all the heads popped off.
I miss how simple life was.

Cracked

How could a pain this deep
have no blood to show for it?
I felt ripped by the seams,
and hung out to dry.
How did this pain
have no scar from the hurt?
No visible evidence to show I was broken.
With cracks so deep they were called
canyons.

Aggression

His hands,
cold and chapped,
wrapped around my wrists
like tape.
Tape that never breaks.
A grip that leaves blue marks
the color of veins.
Veins bulge as the hands
grip tighter.
No words are said.
Just hands are used.
Hands so tight.
Words eliminated.

Warm Sheets

I found comfort in you like I do in
sheets straight from the dryer.
Warm and welcoming.

When We Didn't Know Each Other

It's funny how at one point you barely knew
the person you love at all.
Knowing only their name and their
attractive features.
Not knowing what dreams they wanted to
accomplish of what scared them most.
Then one day you are with them, sharing
chapstick and celebrating each other's
accomplishments.
You have endless amounts of jokes and
nicknames that have crossed borderline obscene.
It's funny that you once tried to always look
beautiful and act polite when they were around.
Now you burp in front of each other and can
wake up and still exchange passionate kisses
with no care if the other's breath hints at late
night Chipotle.

Hell

They say your eyes
are the doorways to
your soul.
And your eyes are
dark,
red,
and probably
just a glimpse
at the hell inside you.

Hate

No I don't hate you,
because hate is a feeling
and I feel nothing for you.

Acknowledgements

First of all, thank you to anyone who reads my book. Whether you came across it by accident, have followed me on my journey of writing or simply were gifted it, I greatly appreciate you spending your time reading the words written on these pages.

Thank you to my family that I love so much for always being supportive so I never felt the need to be a rebellious child.

To my Grandma Du, for giving me so much of your creative genes and constantly lighting up when I talk about my writing with you.

To my best friend since the third grade, Clare. For always being a constant soul in my life and cheering me on in every aspect, no matter how far fetched my ideas are.

To Loren, for being a large reason this book has come to life. My biggest supporter and the best person I know. My love and appreciation for you can't even begin to be put into words.

To anyone who inspired these poems. Thank you fro giving me the ideas, the experience, and the lessons to create and make me into the person I am today.

-Jennae

About The Author

@JennaeCecelia

JennaeCecelia.com

Jeanne Cecelia was born on in St. Paul
Minnesota. Expressing herself through art-
writing, drawing, painting, and photography, has
always been one of her strongest passions. It
allows for her to share her emotions in non-
traditional ways.

Jennae is well known for her poetic soul and
vitality. With years of unpublished work she is
excited about creating ways to further enhance
her reader's experience.
This is her first book.

CPSIA information can be obtained
at www.ICGtesting.com
Printed in the USA
LVOW11s1947170817
545387LV00005B/571/P